calligraphy

MADE EASY:
PROJECT BOOK

BY ASHLEY GARDNER | PRINTABLE WISDOM

Follow us on social media!

Tag us and use #piccadillyinc in your posts
for a chance to win monthly prizes!

This edition published by Piccadilly (USA) Inc.

Piccadilly (USA) Inc.
12702 Via Cortina, Suite 203
Del Mar, CA 92014
USA

10 9 8 7 6 5 4 3 2 1

Printed in China

ISBN-13: 978-1-60863-299-2

MADE EASY:
PROJECT BOOK

Written by Ashley Gardner

Printable Wisdom
PrintableWisdomCo.com

INTRODUCTION

Welcome to the Calligraphy Made Easy Project Book! My name is Ashley Gardner, and together with my husband and business co-founder, I own Printable Wisdom. We started our business, creating hand lettered art and canvas prints, in 2012. Our business is based out of our hometown in Wylie, Texas, and every inch of the walls in our downtown flagship store is covered with hand lettered words turned into works of art.

I first became interested in calligraphy for our designs, when I noticed that using the popular "calligraphy fonts" never gave me exactly the look I was going for. I wanted something completely custom. I wanted to tailor the style and design of the words, to the message they were conveying. I quickly learned that hand lettering each piece was the only way to accomplish this.

So, in the summer of 2012, I browsed blogs and books to try and discover the best path to begin learning this age-old art. I quickly became overwhelmed by the wealth of information available. For months I experimented with various pen and ink types, learning which I enjoyed working with and which made me want to throw away every pen and paper in the house and never pick up a calligraphy pen again! Our kitchen table was regularly littered with endless papers filled with ink splotches and drafts of hand lettered designs.

After years of perfecting my hand lettering technique, I began passing this hard earned knowledge onto others. On social media @PrintableWisdom we regularly post tips for new calligraphers using the hashtag #nofusscalligraphy.

The first "Calligraphy Made Easy" book has all of the instructions and tips needed to make the art of calligraphy more accessible to beginners. In this project book, we will use all of the techniques learned in the first book to have some fun creating hand lettered projects.

By the end of this book, you will learn tons of techniques for transforming your calligraphy from writing into art. Happy lettering!

Ashley Gardner

TRANSFORMING
CALLIGRAPHY INTO ART

This book consists solely of calligraphy projects. The page on the left will have an example project, and the page on the right will be where you create your own works of art.

Each of these projects feature different graphics to combine with your lettering. The instructions will also guide you through various ways to alter your lettering to make beautiful art pieces.

THE PROJECTS

PROJECT #1

Practice writing a single majuscule (capital letter) in the design below.
Use flourishes to fill the space.

You can write a name or word on the banner below—I like combining print
lettering below an ornate letter like this.

PROJECT #2

Practice writing a monogram in this design.

Monograms can consist of either three letters that are all the same size (traditionally in the order of first, middle, last), or with one larger center letter (traditionally in the order of first, last, middle). Try and make your flourishes wrap around the letter(s) beside it to make the monogram look like a finished design.

PROJECT #3

On this project, we will practice making letters look like they are wrapping around an image. To create this effect, part of your word/flourish should be "hidden" behind the image, and part should be written over the top of the image.

PROJECT #4

For this design, choose your favorite miniscule (lowercase) letterform.
Write it in the center of the frame, making sure to balance each side of the
letter so it looks centered in the middle of the composition.

PROJECT #5

For this design, select a short quote or phrase. It may be helpful to sketch the quote in pencil first to make sure everything will fit in this frame. Try to fill as much white space as possible in the frame.

PROJECT #6

This design features a subtle marble background. Practice combining larger calligraphy words with smaller words for a more lengthy quote. This is a great way to emphasize certain words. I like to draw in the large words first, and then fill in the smaller words at the end, making sure that flourishes balance the overall piece.

They tried to bury us; they didn't know we were seeds

MEXICAN PROVERB

PROJECT #7

Monoline calligraphy has become a big trend lately. For this style, you will do the same shape of the letters, but with a stiff pen (any ballpoint pen, or stiff pen will do). There are no thick and thin lines in monoline calligraphy.

For this project, practice writing one word in monoline calligraphy, right above the floral bouquet. It is fine if some of your lettering overlaps onto the bouquet, as long as the word remains readable.

PROJECT #8

This is a combination of projects #6 and #7—we will be writing in a monoline style, with one word larger than the others. Write the word "flowers" first, and fill in the space above and below with the slightly smaller words.

PROJECT #9

Another popular trend in the calligraphy world is "faux-calligraphy." For this style, you will start with a monoline calligraphy design. Then, you will draw in second lines to the left of every downstroke—creating the illusion of thick downstrokes.

For this project, we will leave all lines showing in our "faux" calligraphy.

PROJECT #10

For this project, we are writing a phrase in "faux calligraphy." Start by writing your phrase in monoline calligraphy. Then add in your second lines to the left of every downstroke.

For this example, I've erased lines that cross over my "downstroke" spaces (see red arrow—this line and others like it would be erased).

PROJECT #11

This is just like the last project—faux calligraphy with overlapping lines erased.

Here, we will add stippling to the inside of our faux calligraphy. To do this, start at the bottom of each "downstroke" and make dots very close together. The bottom of each downstroke should almost be solid black.

As you move up, make the dots further and further apart. This creates a glitter or confetti effect inside your lettering.

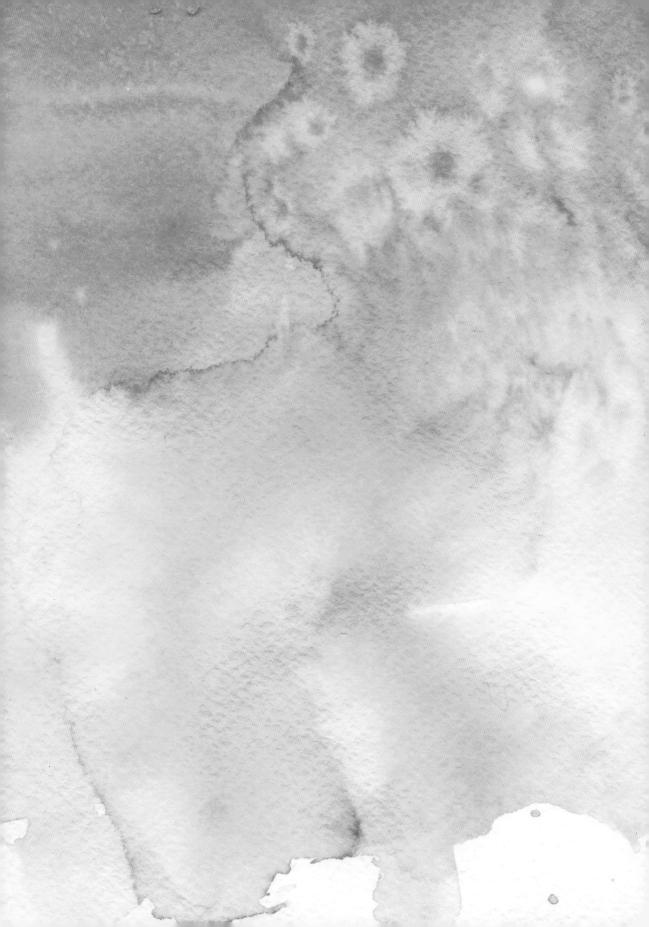

PROJECT #12

Here, we are getting back to our standard calligraphy. Choose a word that you can create flourishes on the top and bottom of. You may want to have a "t" included for the top flourish, and letters such as "g", "y", "j" or "p" for the bottom flourish.

Now, write your word so that the top and bottom flourishes balance each other out.

PROJECT #13

For this project, you will write your lettering in "faux" calligraphy. Then, fill in each downstroke except for the pattern shown in this example. You will have a long white space at the top of each downstroke, with two small white dots below it. This creates a shadowing effect.

PROJECT #14

For this project, all words are written on one baseline. I chose a quote with a lot of "t" letterforms to show how you can use the crossbar on the "t" to fill in white space. Try your hand at writing this quote on the next page, adding the crossbars at the very end to fill in any extra white space in your composition.

PROJECT #15

Filling a space evenly with lettering can be a difficult skill to learn. Start by writing your phrase in pencil, and adding swirls and flourishes to fill in negative space. Plan where each word will fit in, and try to make all of your words the same general size.

PROJECT #16

The connections between your letters are called "transitions."
Transitions can be smooth, as shown below.

To practice this technique, avoid any sharp points in your lettering—the entire
word can be written in only one stroke, with no breaks.

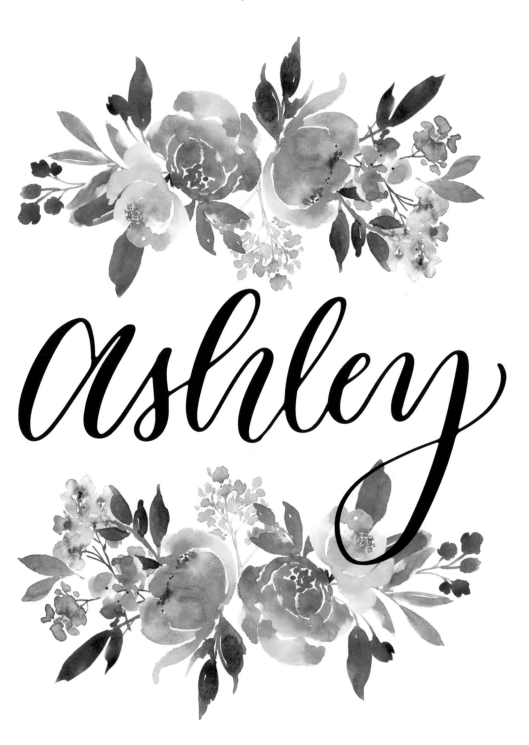

PROJECT #17

The alternative to smooth transitions are sharp transitions as shown here.
Each letter ends in a sharp point before you continue on to the next letterform.

You should pick your pen up in between each stroke when drawing sharp transitions
in order to accentuate the angles.

PROJECT #18

Combining print and calligraphy is ideal for long quotes. In this design, write the quote from top to bottom, filling in spaces between the larger calligraphy words with smaller print words.

LET YOUR *dreams* BE BIGGER THAN YOUR *fears*, YOUR *actions* LOUDER THAN YOUR *words*, AND YOUR STRONGER *faith* THAN YOUR *feelings*

PROJECT #19

Often, an ampersand fits into a design more neatly than writing the word "and."
Below, is an ornate ampersand, written in the style of a wedding invitation or decoration.
For this design, write the ampersand first in the center of the page, then write a name
above with a curve to it, followed by a name below with the opposite curve.

PROJECT #20

Flourishes are a great way to connect words in a design!
The best way to create this fluid look is to draw your letters in pencil first, to plan where
the flourishes will connect. The letter "t" is always a great choice for adding a flourish.

PROJECT #21

Below is an example of a wedding invitation. On the next page, choose two names (first names only or first and last names) to write in the spaces provided.

Calligraphy with a bit of a bouncy baseline is a nice match to the subdued sans-serif font included on the invitation.

YOU ARE INVITED TO JOIN US
IN CELEBRATING THE MARRIAGE OF

Emily Pearson

TO

Michael Smith

ON SATURDAY, THE FIFTH OF JUNE
TWO-THOUSAND SEVENTEEN
AT SIX O'CLOCK IN THE EVENING

HICKORY COUNTRY CLUB
1489 HICKORY CREEK ROAD
DALLAS, TEXAS 75091

YOU ARE INVITED TO JOIN US
IN CELEBRATING THE MARRIAGE OF

TO

ON SATURDAY, THE FIFTH OF JUNE
TWO-THOUSAND SEVENTEEN
AT SIX O'CLOCK IN THE EVENING

HICKORY COUNTRY CLUB
1489 HICKORY CREEK ROAD
DALLAS, TEXAS 75091

PROJECT #22

Addressing envelopes is one of the best ways to utilize your new calligraphy skill!

For this envelope style, the name is larger and written in modern calligraphy.
Below, the address lines are written in a simple block font.

PROJECT #23

This project features a seating placecard—popular at formal wedding dinners.

Generally on placecards you want to make sure that the name is readable from a distance—a good way to ensure this is to make the first letters of each name larger and distinctive. This helps people spot their place more easily from across the room.

PROJECT #24

Here, we will practice lettering a menu.

The title and subheadings of this menu are written in modern calligraphy,
with a very simple sans serif font beneath the subheadings.

To get nice straight lines, lightly use a ruler and pencil to draw guides.
Erase the guides when you have completed the project.

Menu

starter

RAW OYSTERS
WITH GARLIC GLAZE

entreé

ROASTED LAMB
WITH MINT SAUCE

dessert

HOMEMADE APPLE PIE
WITH ICE CREAM

PROJECT #25

Another more modern way of addressing an envelope is to fill the entire paper with your recipient's name and address.

Use a bouncy baseline for your calligraphy here, and don't be afraid to vary the size of the letters and numbers to fill in all of the negative space on the front of the envelope.

PROJECT #26

Choosing a design to accompany your calligraphy is key—this quote not only fits perfectly in the floral frame, but the content of the quote matches the motif as well.

PROJECT #27

This design focuses all of the attention on a super-flourished capital "B."
Choose a quote that starts with your favorite majescule and add flourishes
to make it the star of the show in this project.

PROJECT #28

This style of addressing envelopes is more classic than the previous projects.

For this design, every line will be written in calligraphy. Vary the size of the text on each line, so that all of the three lines take up approximately the same amount of space on the envelope. I.e. if the name is shorter (as shown here) it will need to be larger to take up the same amount of space as the line below it. Longer names will need to be smaller.

PROJECT #29

This is a variation of the prior project, but with a curved baseline for each line of the address. To accomplish this, write three wavy lines in pencil. Each line should have a slight "S" shape.

Then, write your address using the pencil lines as your baseline. Erase the pencil marks when you are done, and your address will have a nice gentle curve to it.

PROJECT #30

Here, we will fill a circle with a short quote or phrase.

If you need to have some letters overlap the design (like the "c" in "come" shown here),
then make sure to overlap on light colored portions of the design,
so that readability is not impaired.

PROJECT #31

Here, we are adding majuscules in to the middle of a quote for emphasis on certain words. The "R", "B", and "A" all fall in the middle of the quote, but when we capitalize them, they draw the eye to these portions of the design. Write the three large words first, and then fill in the spaces with a combination of print and smaller calligraphy words.

PROJECT #32

Adding simple illustrations to a design is a great way to turn simple lettering into a work of art. Write the following quote first—drawing the words "Follow" and "Dreams" at the beginning, and filling in the middle space with the word "your."

Then, draw two lines for your arrows, leaving enough room for their tails. You can embellish the tails any way you want—add patterns, dots, stripes, or flourishes!

PROJECT #33

Here we are writing a quote in a freeform arrangement. There aren't any borders to constrain the design, so we can be a little more creative with the way we arrange the letters.

In the example below, I chose to give my composition a rounded square shape—you can arrange your text to be more circular, rectangular, or spread out than this depending on the look you would like for your project.

PROJECT #34

Monoline calligraphy looks great on a single baseline, which we will practice below.

To get straight baselines, draw guides with a ruler and pencil, making sure to draw the lines equidistant from each other.

And still I will rise.

Maya Angelou

PROJECT #35

You can switch up the look of your calligraphy easily by varying the amount of pressure you apply on your downstrokes.

Here, I only slightly increased the pressure during downstrokes, making these lines only slightly thicker than the thin upstrokes. This gives a loose and flowing look to the piece.

PROJECT #36

In an irregularly shaped design, it's important to plan where each of your words will fit. Here, the quote starts on the top left of the oval, and each line slightly shifts, to end at the bottom right of the oval.

Never ever ever give up

PROJECT #37

Large serif print is becoming more and more popular in the hand lettering world!

For this design, write "LOVE" and "LIFE" first.
Then, fill in the spaces with the calligraphy lettering.

Add serifs (the little "feet" on the capital letters) to the printed letters.

PROJECT #38

For this design, we fill in negative space and balance the composition with flourishes. Any letters with a descender are perfect for adding an extra flourish in—like the "g" shown here.

Sometimes, I will leave the tail of the descender off of the letter until the entire composition is done, and add in the tail of the "g" as the very last step. This way you ensure that you have filled in all of the negative space.

PROJECT #39

In this project, we combine serif lettering and bold "faux" calligraphy. Write the word "bravely" with thick downstrokes, and then add lines to the left of each downstroke last, giving your lettering a bold "faux" calligraphy look as we have practiced earlier.

PROJECT #40

This composition makes the capital letter "P" the star of the show.
Write the words "Prove" and "Wrong" first, leaving enough room for the middle word.

Then, write the word "them" and add your flourish through the center of the composition.

PROJECT #41

If your calligraphy pen isn't super thick, you can still get a thick downstroke by going over each downstroke a second time. Here, write the entire composition and then go back and make each downstroke doubly-thick.

PROJECT #42

In this project, we focus on making each vowel very small in comparison to the other letters around them. This is a great way to make your lettering look "modern" but still follow a general rule so it doesn't get too out of control!

P R O J E C T   # 4 3

In this project, use the "faux calligraphy" technique on your print letters! Add in a downstroke line, leaving a space between each downstroke as shown below.

PROJECT #44

Here, we will practice drawing a simple curved banner!

Draw two parallel "S" curved lines

Connect the lines with two vertical lines

Add in a "C" shape and a straight line on each end as shown here

Draw a "V" on each end and a vertical line for the back of the banner

PROJECT #45

Now, practice drawing a banner centered underneath this home illustration.

After you have drawn your banner, plan the text you will write inside, making sure to center the text and follow the curve of the banner.

PROJECT #46

This is a more complicated piece, requiring a lot of planning to fill in all of the space available. I recommend writing your quote in pencil first, to make sure that you don't run out of room, or have too much white space at the end. Fill in the edges with flourishes to balance the piece.

Amazing grace, how sweet the sound that saved a wretch like me. I once was lost but now I'm found, was blind but now I see.

PROJECT #47

We have practiced filling in circular and rectangular designs with our lettering—now we can take it to the next level by filling in a diamond shaped space! Start with just a single word on the first line, and end with either a single word on the last line, or a flourish that descends into the bottom point as shown in this example.

PROJECT #48

Here, we fill in a large negative space with a heavily flourished "y" in "Beauty."

We also have words intersecting ("Beauty" and "for"). To make sure that this doesn't affect the readability of the piece, leave small spaces where the lines intersect as shown here.

PROJECT #49

Sometimes a straight baseline is the best technique for simple pieces.

We add to the visual interest of this composition by varying the size of the words on each line—making "every day" much larger than the three lines prior to these words.

PROJECT #50

Adding visual interest to a single word written in calligraphy can be difficult at times.

Here, we make the word "Love" a bit more interesting by connecting the first and last letters. To do this, write the letters "ov" first. Then, add in the L with a sweeping flourish underneath "ov" and add an "e" at the end of the word.

This may be easier to practice in pencil a few times first to master the technique.

PROJECT #51

Here we are creating an entire composition from scratch!

Draw the banner first, adding shading to the "back" portion of the banner as shown.
Then, write the word "YOUR" in simple block lettering,
with thick downstrokes and thin upstrokes.

Write the word "Bless" above the banner, and "heart" below the banner. Make sure to
center these to give your entire composition a balanced shape.

P R O J E C T   # 5 2

In this project, we are making one of the words of our composition bold.

To do this, write your entire composition once. Then, go over the downstrokes
in the word "got" for a second time—making them doubly thick.

This would be a great piece to get creative with your flourishes on the following letters:
Y, T, G, T

PROJECT #53

For this design, we are using only monoline calligraphy with a very thin pen.
A standard ball point pen would work great for this project!

For a lengthy quote, I generally always pencil in a plan for where
each word will go before inking my design.

PROJECT #54

Writing on an angled baseline can seem tricky at first—and beginners may prefer to simply turn the book pages to write this word angled up and to the right.

However, it gives a different look if you can keep the book straight and write at this angled baseline. This is a great way to focus on the letterforms and discover new and interesting ways to write letters if you are in a rut.

PROJECT #55

Faux calligraphy adds a lot of visual interest to a monoline majuscule letter!

First, write your letter in monoline calligraphy and make sure to add lots of flourishes.
Then, use the "faux calligraphy" technique to add a thick downstroke where it is needed.

PROJECT #56

Filling a space with a short quote can be just as challenging as writing a long quote in the same space. Instead of filling every corner with words, you have to use flourishes to fill in the corners.

Here, we use flourishes on the "y" descender. We also add a flourish to our "r" which is a non-standard flourish, but adds a lot of visual interest!

To make sure that readability isn't affected, I like to make sure that all flourishes (especially non-standard flourishes) are only thin strokes, with no thick lines.

PROJECT #57

On this project, we are using another 'non-standard' flourish on our "s."

Again, we see how this flourish is only thin lines. This makes it clear to the reader that this last letter is an "s" and that the swoop above is only for decoration and is not part of the word to be read.

PROJECT #58

Sometimes a space in a design is too irregular to fit our quote in!

For this situation, make sure that you overlap your words on light portions of the design (like the light pink flower shown here).

Overlapping on dark portions will make your piece difficult and cumbersome to read.

here comes the sun!

PROJECT #59

Here, we add a banner in the middle of a wreath. Draw your banner first, making sure to center it in the composition. Add shading to the back of the banner if you would like.

Next, write the word "your" in the banner, making sure to stay within the lines and follow the curve of the banner.

Write the words "DO" and "BEST" above and below the banner, making sure your downstrokes are thick and upstrokes are thin.

PROJECT #60

This banner is a slightly different variation of previous ones we have drawn. Instead of starting with two "S" curves, start with two parallel "C" curves.

Then, follow the same techniques to create the tails of your banner as shown below.

When writing "to come" beneath the banner, you can use the flourish on your "t" to fill in negative space under the C-shaped banner.

PROJECT #61

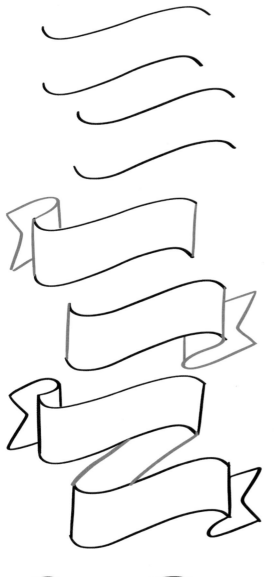

To draw a double banner, start by drawing two sets of parallel "S" curved lines.

Then, add a tail to the left of the top banner, and a tail to the right of the bottom banner. Instead of adding tails to the other ends, however, just draw a straight line.

Then, draw two parallel straight lines connecting the top and bottom banner as shown here.

You can add shading to the "back" portions of the banner, as well!

PROJECT #62

This project focuses on combining print majuscule letterforms with calligraphy miniscule letterforms. Each of the lines begins with a capital letter written in print with some flourishes added. Then, write the remainder of each line in calligraphy with a bouncy baseline.

PROJECT #63

For this project, the last word is centered over the watercolor swash.

Write the last word first, in all capital letters and wait until the
very end to add the flourish on the "T" crossbar.

Write the words in calligraphy above "ALRIGHT" and then finally add
in the flourish on the capital T to fill in any blank spaces.

PROJECT #64

Again, we are using majuscule letterforms on each line to add visual interest to this piece.
Notice how each line starts off center, in order to fill in the blank space evenly.

PROJECT #65

For this design, start by drawing a double banner. Then, fill in the words
"WORK" and "AND BE" as shown.

For the last step, write "hard" and "kind" in calligraphy on the banner.

PROJECT #66

Print letters can be flourished as well! On this design, the uppercase "L" in "welcome" has a simple flourish to underline the letters "C" and "O."

The word "home" has opening and ending flourishes to balance out the top and bottom lines on this piece.

PROJECT #67

Adding calligraphy to an illustration can be difficult, because you want to add balance to the overall piece with the placement of your letters.

Here, we use very ornate majuscule letters on each line, and make the entire lettering portion angle to the right. This balances the illustration which is placed on the left side of the page.

PROJECT #68

It can be fun to write words in an illustrative way such as this. Start by writing the word "raindrops" on the center of the page. Then, add tiny teardrop shapes on low points of the word, as if they are dripping off of your lettering.

P R O J E C T   # 6 9

Almost any writing tool can be used to create calligraphy!
Here, I used a pencil with a sharp tip. Make sure to hold the pencil at a
45 degree angle in order to get your thick and thin strokes.

For a finishing touch, I added in a second line to the left of each downstroke
(similar to when we did "faux calligraphy" earlier).

PROJECT #70

Here, we create another piece with a sharp pencil—any type will do!

PROJECT #71

This design has flourishes galore! Start by writing a capital "F" and adding ornate flourishes to the top crossbar. Then, write "lour" adding a descending flourish to the lowercase "r" as shown. Next we will write "is"—make sure to stop after writing the "s." For this "h" you will start at the fourish on top, then make your "h" connect to the line coming off of the "s." Finally, end with a descending flourish on the "h."

PROJECT #72

This word is written much differently than the last one, while still having a lot of flourishes and visual interest.

Start by writing this print "F" with a flourish on the crossbar. Then, write "louris" and finish with the "h" (starting with the flourish portion as before).

PROJECT #73

On this piece, we can practice more ornate flourishes on the "t" and "y" letterforms.
I like to wait until the entire piece is written (leaving out the flourishes) and then adding
those in at the very last step in order to ensure balance in the finished composition.

PROJECT #74

Here we create very bold calligraphy. You may need to go over each line many times depending on the thickness of your calligraphy pen. Lastly, add in the decorative "starburst" elements as shown, having them taper in as you get closer to the lettering.

PROJECT #75

This casual calligraphy style is one of my favorites.

To master this look, use your calligraphy pen but do not apply any extra pressure on the downstrokes. You will get a not-quite-monoline looking text when you are finished, making the script look casual and effortless.

PROJECT #76

Here, we use a thick line for the crossbar on the "t" in "another."

I usually only use this technique in short quotes such as this. Using a thick crossbar can make the text difficult to read if it is very long, but is a great technique to use for short phrases.

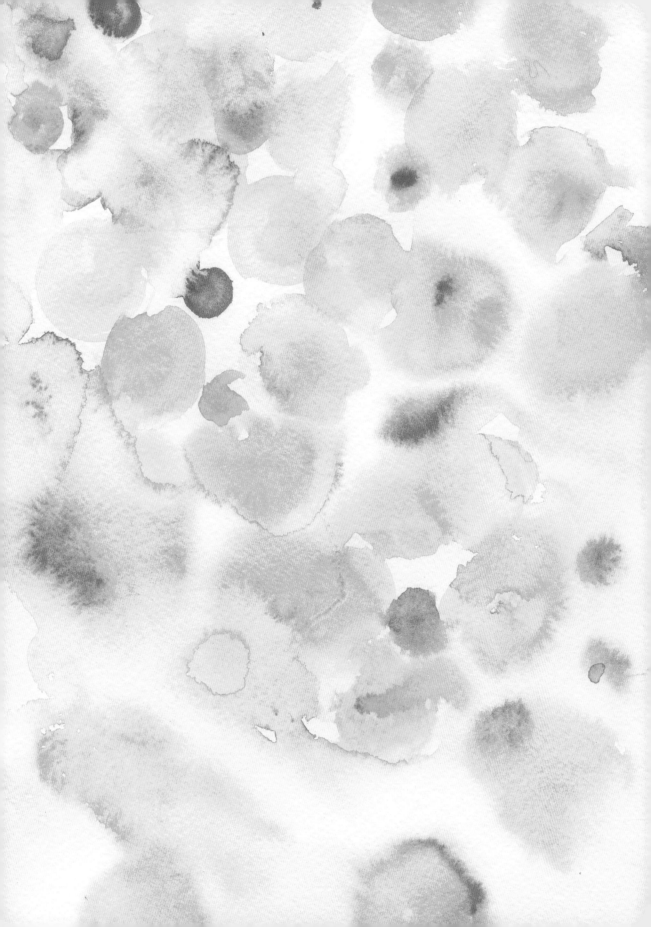

PROJECT #77

This piece has four ornate majuscule letterforms. I chose to write each letter in this style with a curl at the bottom left to help with readability. Making your flourishes similar in each letter such as this will make it easier for others to read your text. The flourish on the "t" in "the" was added as a last step in order to balance out the overall composition.

PROJECT #78

Here, the flourish on the "t" is drawn to connect with the lowercase "d" in "outside." Connecting flourishes like this is a great way to fill in negative space in your work!

PROJECT #79

Here we combine bold print script (with a shadow added for emphasis) and flowing calligraphy with tons of flourishes.

This quote was chosen specifically because we can echo the sentiment (i.e. "WORK HARD" is written in a bold and no nonsense font while "and be kind" is a gentler font) of the quote in the style of calligraphy we use.

PROJECT #80

For this design, use monoline calligraphy (any felt tipped pen will work!).
The ampersand is added as a last step to fill in the space underneath the word "sparkle."

P R O J E C T   # 8 1

Combining calligraphy with different baseline structures can be a
great way to add visual interest to a piece.

Here, we are using a stable baseline for the words "do something." All letters sit on one
line. Then, the word "unexpected" is written with a varying or "bouncy" baseline.

PROJECT #82

On this project, we are adding three ornate flourishes—after the word is written.

Write the entire word, leaving out the flourishes. Then, it can be useful to plan where your flourishes will go with a pencil to make sure that the overall piece is balanced. You'll want plenty of flourishes on the top and bottom of your word.

PROJECT #83

Here, we will add color to our calligraphy!

Start by writing the quote of your choice in "faux calligraphy" as we have practiced before.
Then, erase all of the overlapping lines.

Take colored pencils and color in the "spaces" in your faux calligraphy.
Here, I used colored pencils all in shades of blue.

Looking for more?

Similar titles available by Piccadilly:

300 Drawing Prompts

500 Drawing Prompts

Calligraphy Made Easy

Comic Sketchbook

Sketching Made Easy

300 Writing Prompts

300 MORE Writing Prompts

500 Writing Prompts

3000 Questions About Me

3000 Would You Rather Questions

Choose Your Own Journal

Complete the Story

Your Father's Story

Your Mother's Story

The Story of My Life

Write the Story

100 Life Challenges

Awesome Social Media Quizzes

Find the Cat

Find 2 Cats

Time Capsule Letters

WWW.PICCADILLYINC.COM